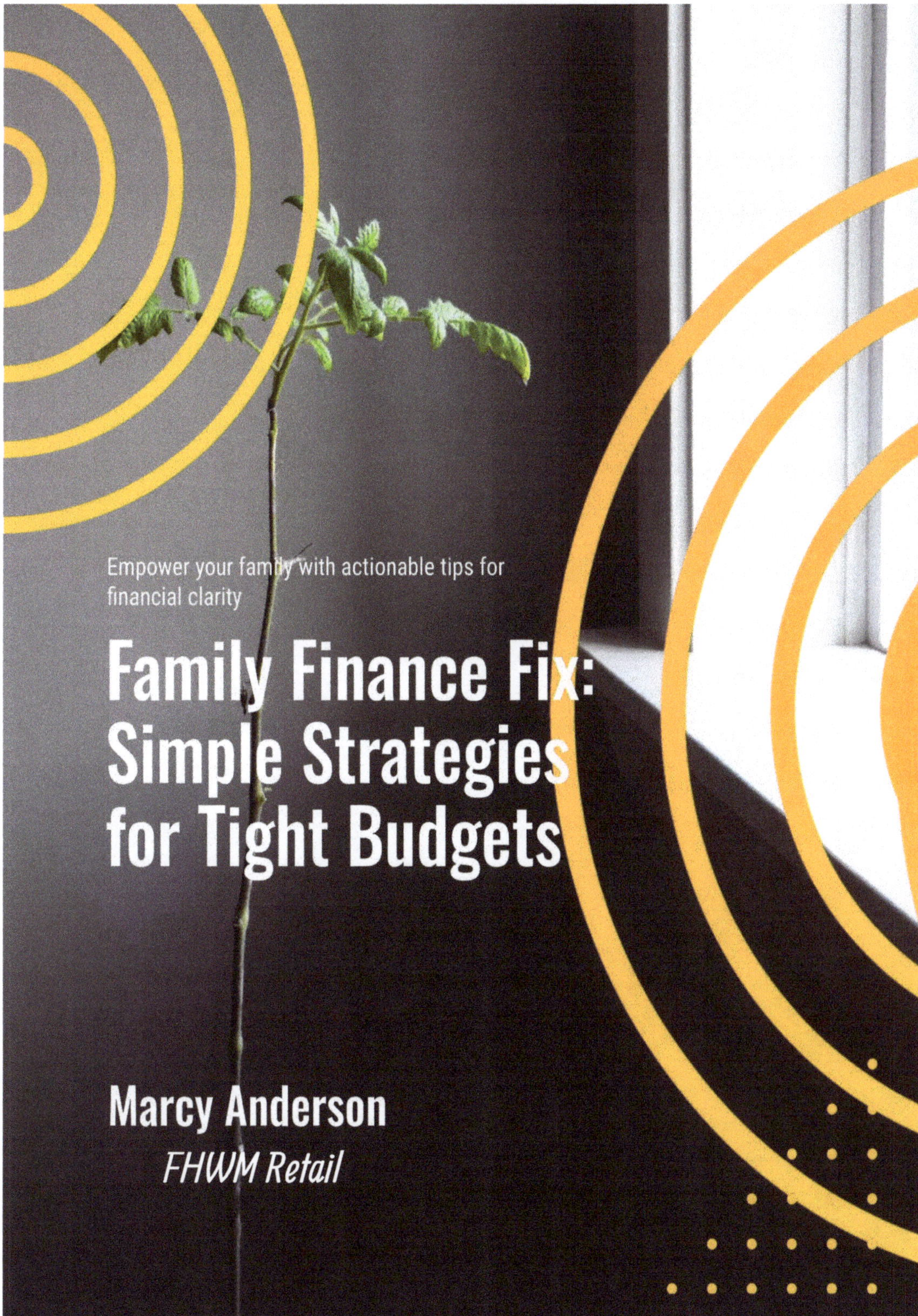

Empower your family with actionable tips for financial clarity

Family Finance Fix: Simple Strategies for Tight Budgets

Marcy Anderson

FHWM Retail

Table Of Contents

01

Chapter 1: Understanding Family Finances

The Importance of Financial Literacy

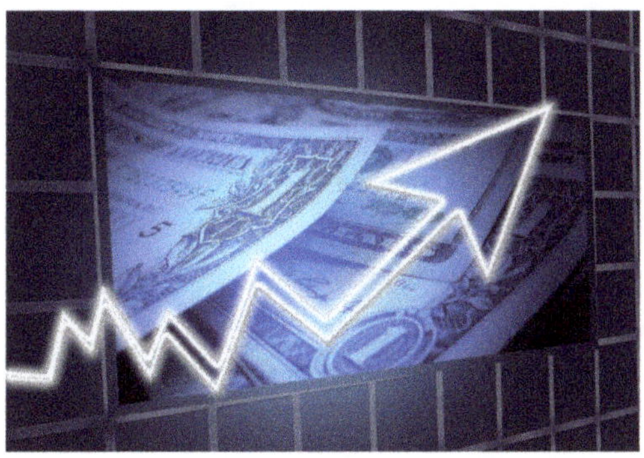

Financial literacy is a crucial skill that can empower individuals and families to navigate the complexities of modern financial life. In times of economic hardship, understanding basic financial concepts becomes even more vital. Knowledge of budgeting, saving, and investing can help families make informed decisions that lead to better financial outcomes. By equipping themselves with this knowledge, families can take control of their finances and work towards achieving stability, even in challenging circumstances.

One of the most significant benefits of financial literacy is its role in effective budgeting. Families facing financial distress often have limited resources, making it essential to allocate every dollar wisely. By learning how to create and maintain a budget, families can identify their essential expenses, cut unnecessary costs, and prioritize savings. This disciplined approach not only helps in managing day-to-day expenses but also provides a clear roadmap for achieving long-term financial goals.

Emergency savings plans are another key component of financial literacy. Families need to be prepared for unexpected expenses, such as medical emergencies or car repairs, which can derail their financial stability. Understanding how to set aside funds for these occasions can bring peace of mind and reduce stress. Financial literacy encourages families to establish a safety net, ensuring that they are not solely reliant on credit options, which can lead to further debt.

Reducing household debt is a common concern for many families, and financial literacy offers strategies to tackle this issue effectively. By learning about interest rates, repayment options, and debt management techniques, families can develop a plan to pay off their debts systematically. This knowledge empowers them to make informed decisions about borrowing and helps prevent the cycle of debt that many find themselves trapped in.

Finally, financial literacy extends to practical aspects of daily living, such as meal planning and generating home-based income. Families can benefit from learning how to create nutritious, cost-effective meals that fit their budgets. Additionally, exploring ideas for home-based income generation can provide families with the extra financial cushion they need. By embracing sustainable living practices and reducing household costs, families can build a more resilient financial future, ensuring that they are better prepared for whatever challenges may arise.

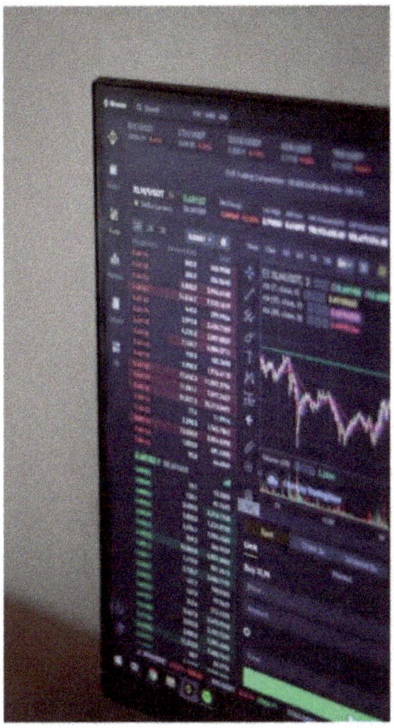

Identifying your financial goals is the first step towards achieving financial stability, especially for families facing economic hardship. It involves a thorough assessment of your current financial situation, including income, expenses, and debts. By understanding where you stand financially, you can set realistic and achievable goals that cater to your specific needs and circumstances. Whether it's saving for a rainy day or planning for retirement, having clear objectives is essential in navigating tough financial times.

Identifying Your Financial Goals

One effective method for goal identification is the SMART criteria that we also use in the medical field, which stands for Specific, Measurable, Achievable, Relevant, and Time-bound. This framework helps families articulate their financial aspirations more clearly. For instance, instead of vaguely stating, "I want to save money," a SMART goal would be, "I aim to save $500 for emergencies within six months." This specificity not only makes the goal more attainable but also provides a tangible target to work towards.

Another vital aspect of identifying financial goals is prioritization. Families should differentiate between short-term and long-term goals. Short-term goals may include paying off small debts or saving for a family event, while long-term goals could encompass saving for a child's education or retirement. By categorizing these goals, families can allocate their resources more effectively, ensuring that immediate needs are addressed while still planning for the future.

Additionally, it is crucial to involve all family members in the goal-setting process, especially in households with children or elderly members. This inclusivity fosters a sense of responsibility and teamwork. By discussing financial goals openly, families can collectively brainstorm strategies to achieve them, such as budgeting together or finding ways to cut costs on everyday expenses. This collaborative approach not only strengthens family bonds but also enhances the effectiveness of the financial plan.

Finally, regularly revisiting and adjusting financial goals is essential. Life circumstances can change rapidly, and what may have been an important goal six months ago might no longer hold the same weight. Families should review their goals periodically and make necessary adjustments based on changes in income, expenses, or family dynamics. This flexibility is key to maintaining financial health and ensuring that the family can adapt to new challenges as they arise.

Assessing Your Current Financial Situation

Assessing your current financial situation is the first and most crucial step in regaining control over your household finances. Begin by gathering all relevant financial documents, including bank statements, bills, and pay stubs. This comprehensive overview will help you understand your income sources, regular expenses, and any outstanding debts. By having a clear picture of your finances, you can identify areas that need immediate attention and develop a strategy to address them.

Next, it's important to categorize your expenses into fixed and variable costs. Fixed expenses, such as rent or mortgage payments, remain constant each month, while variable expenses, such as groceries and entertainment, can fluctuate. By breaking down your spending, you can pinpoint areas where you can cut back and allocate more funds towards essentials or savings. This categorisation also aids in creating a realistic budget tailored to your family's needs.

Another vital aspect of assessing your financial situation is evaluating your debt. List all debts, including credit cards, loans, and any other obligations, noting the interest rates and minimum payments. Understanding the total amount you owe and the cost of maintaining these debts enables you to prioritize repayment strategies. Consider focusing on high-interest debts first, as these can significantly impact your overall financial health.

Additionally, assess your emergency savings. Ideally, families should aim to have at least three to six months' worth of living expenses saved for unforeseen circumstances. If your savings are lacking, explore ways to build this safety net, such as automating transfers to a savings account or cutting back on non-essential spending and getting a temporary/seasonal job to add to this fund. Having an emergency fund provides peace of mind and can prevent you from falling deeper into debt during tough times.

Finally, consider alternative income sources to improve your financial situation. This may involve exploring home-based income generation ideas, such as freelancing or starting a small business. By diversifying your income streams, you can increase your financial stability and create more opportunities for savings and debt repayment. The combination of assessing your current financial situation and implementing strategic changes will empower you to navigate through economic hardship successfully.

Learn to take a fun hobby and create an income stream.

02

Chapter 2: Budgeting Strategies for Families in Financial Distress

Creating a Realistic Family Budget

Family Finance Fix: Simple Strategies for Tight Budgets

Creating a realistic family budget is essential for families facing economic hardship. The first step involves evaluating your current financial situation by listing all sources of income and expenses. This includes fixed costs like rent or mortgage payments, utilities, and groceries, as well as variable costs such as entertainment and dining out. By having a clear picture of your finances, you can identify areas where adjustments can be made to ensure that your budget aligns with your financial goals.

Once you have assessed your income and expenses, the next step is to prioritize your spending. Distinguish between needs and wants, focusing on essential expenses first. For instance, housing, food, and healthcare are priorities that must be funded before discretionary spending. By prioritizing your budget, you can allocate your resources more effectively, ensuring that your family's basic needs are met while reducing unnecessary expenditures.

In addition to prioritizing your spending, setting specific savings goals is crucial. Establishing an emergency savings fund can provide a safety net during unexpected financial challenges. Aim to save at least three to six months' worth of living expenses, starting with small, manageable amounts. Automating your savings can also help, as it makes the process easier and ensures that you consistently set money aside for future needs.

Moreover, consider implementing strategies to reduce household debt. This may involve consolidating loans, negotiating with creditors, or exploring community resources for financial assistance. Reducing debt not only improves your financial health but also alleviates stress, allowing families to focus on building a more secure financial future. Developing a plan to pay down debt should be a key component of your budgeting strategy.

Lastly, meal planning can significantly cut costs and contribute to effective budgeting. By planning meals in advance, families can avoid impulse purchases and reduce food waste. Consider incorporating more home-cooked meals into your routine, as this can be both cost-effective and healthier. Additionally, exploring home-based income generation ideas can bolster your budget, allowing for greater financial stability. Embracing sustainable living practices can further reduce household costs and create a more resilient family budget.

How can everyone cut costs daily, weekly, monthly?

ΣΥΝΟΛΟ
ΜΕΤΡΗΤΑ
ΡΕΣΤΑ
* ΕΥΧΑΡΙΣΤΟΥΜΕ *

25%
OFF

It's easy to grow celery & mint.

Tracking Income and Expenses

Tracking income and expenses is a crucial step for families facing economic hardship. Understanding where your money comes from and where it goes can provide clarity and empower you to make informed financial decisions. By keeping a detailed record of all income sources, whether from jobs, benefits, or side hustles, families can paint a comprehensive picture of their financial situation. This transparency is essential for budgeting effectively and identifying areas where spending can be reduced.

To start tracking income and expenses, families can utilize simple tools such as spreadsheets or budgeting apps. These tools can help organize financial information and offer visual insights into spending habits. Regularly updating this information allows families to spot trends and make adjustments as needed. Additionally, establishing a routine for reviewing finances, perhaps weekly or monthly, can reinforce the importance of managing household finances and encourage accountability within the family.

One effective strategy is to categorize expenses into fixed and variable costs. Fixed costs, such as rent or mortgage payments, are often non-negotiable, while variable costs, like groceries and entertainment, provide more flexibility. By analyzing variable expenses, families can identify areas for potential savings. For instance, opting for meal planning can not only reduce grocery bills but also promote healthier eating habits, further enhancing financial and physical well-being.

Emergency savings plans are also an essential component of financial tracking. Even small contributions to a savings account can build a safety net over time, providing peace of mind in case of unexpected expenses. Families can set specific savings goals, such as covering three months' worth of living expenses, and track progress alongside regular income and expenditure monitoring. This proactive approach can help families feel more secure in their financial situation.

Lastly, reducing household debt is a vital goal for families in distress. By keeping meticulous records of all debts, including interest rates and repayment schedules, families can prioritize which debts to tackle first. Strategies such as the snowball method, where smaller debts are paid off first, can provide quick wins and motivation. Maintaining a clear understanding of financial obligations, alongside tracking income and expenses, is key to achieving long-term financial stability and resilience.

Prioritizing Essential Spending

In times of economic hardship, prioritizing essential spending becomes an essential skill for families striving to make ends meet. It involves distinguishing between needs and wants, allowing households to channel their limited resources towards necessities such as food, housing, and healthcare. By creating a clear list of essential expenses, families can gain a better understanding of their financial priorities and make informed decisions about their spending habits.

One effective strategy is to develop a monthly budget that allocates funds specifically for essential items. This budget should reflect realistic figures based on past spending patterns and current financial capabilities. By tracking expenditures, families can identify areas where they may be overspending or where adjustments can be made. This proactive approach not only helps in managing immediate financial challenges but also sets a solid foundation for long-term financial stability.

Meal planning is another crucial aspect of prioritizing essential spending. Families can save significant amounts by planning their meals for the week, using ingredients that are both cost-effective and nutritious. By preparing a shopping list based on the meal plan, unnecessary purchases can be avoided, thus ensuring that funds are spent wisely. This not only supports the household budget but also promotes healthier eating habits, which can lead to long-term health benefits.

Additionally, exploring home-based income generation ideas can provide families with extra financial support. This could involve utilizing skills such as crafting, baking, photography, art or even offering online tutoring services. Such initiatives not only create additional income but also foster a sense of purpose and engagement within the family unit. Even small earnings can make a significant difference in easing financial burdens.

Finally, sustainable living practices can contribute to reducing household costs. Simple changes such as conserving energy, reducing waste, and opting for second-hand items can lead to substantial savings over time. By adopting a mindset focused on sustainability, families not only prioritize essential spending but also create a more resilient and eco-friendly household. This holistic approach to managing finances can empower families to navigate financial distress more effectively, ensuring their basic needs are met while fostering a culture of resourcefulness and responsibility.

SPEND

03

Chapter 3: Building an Emergency Savings Plan

The Necessity of an Emergency Fund

In today's uncertain economic climate, the necessity of having an emergency fund cannot be overstated. Families across the United States are facing unprecedented challenges, and financial distress is a reality for many. An emergency fund acts as a safety net, providing crucial support during unexpected events such as job loss, medical emergencies, or urgent home repairs. Without it, families may find themselves in a cycle of debt, exacerbating their financial difficulties.

Establishing an emergency fund starts with budgeting effectively. Families should assess their monthly expenses and identify areas where they can cut back. This could involve meal planning to reduce grocery bills or finding ways to generate income from home, such as freelancing or selling handmade goods. By reallocating these savings into an emergency fund, families can gradually build a cushion that will afford them peace of mind in times of crisis.

The recommended amount for an emergency fund varies, but a common guideline is to save at least three to six months' worth of living expenses. This amount may seem daunting, but families can reach this goal by setting achievable milestones. For instance, starting with a target of $500 can provide initial relief, and from there, families can work towards larger savings. The key is consistency and commitment, ensuring that contributions to the fund become a regular part of the budgeting strategy.

In addition to savings, families should consider strategies for reducing household debt. High levels of debt can hinder the ability to save effectively, making it essential to address this issue simultaneously. Consolidating debts, negotiating lower interest rates, or seeking assistance from financial advisors can help families regain control over their finances. By reducing debt, families free up more resources to contribute to their emergency fund.

Ultimately, the goal of an emergency fund is not only to survive financial hardship but to thrive in spite of it. By preparing for the unexpected, families can navigate challenges with confidence and stability. The journey to financial security may be long, but with careful planning and disciplined saving, families can achieve their financial goals and reduce the stress associated with economic uncertainty.

How Much Should You Save?

Saving money can seem daunting, especially for families facing economic hardship. However, establishing a savings plan is essential for financial stability and peace of mind. Start by assessing your current financial situation, including income, expenses, and any outstanding debts. This understanding will provide a foundation for determining how much you can realistically set aside each month. Even small amounts can accumulate over time and make a significant difference in times of crisis.

Aim to create an emergency savings fund that covers at least three to six months of living expenses. This fund can be a financial safety net during unexpected situations such as job loss or medical emergencies. To build this fund, consider setting aside a specific percentage of your income each month, even if it's just a modest sum. Additionally, automating your savings by directing a portion of your paycheck into a separate savings account can help make saving easier and more consistent.

In order to save effectively, it's essential to evaluate your monthly budget and identify areas where you can reduce spending. Look for non-essential expenses that can be trimmed or eliminated altogether. For instance, consider meal planning to reduce grocery bills or seeking out free community resources for entertainment. These adjustments not only free up funds for savings but also encourage a more mindful approach to spending.

Another vital strategy is to prioritize paying down high-interest debts. Reducing debt not only improves your financial health but also makes it easier to save money in the long run. Consider consolidating debts or negotiating lower interest rates with creditors. By decreasing the amount you owe, you'll have more resources available to contribute to your savings, allowing you to build a more secure financial future for your family.

Lastly, explore alternative income generation ideas that can supplement your household budget. This could involve taking on part-time work, freelancing, or starting a small home-based business. Engaging in these activities not only brings in extra money but can also lead to skills development and increased self-sufficiency. Embracing sustainable living practices, such as growing your own vegetables or reducing energy consumption, can further cut household costs and contribute to your savings efforts.

Strategies for Building Savings Quickly

Building savings quickly is crucial for families facing economic hardship. One effective strategy is to create a budget that prioritizes essential expenses while identifying areas where spending can be reduced. By tracking every expense and categorizing them into needs and wants, families can uncover opportunities to cut back, which can ultimately lead to increased savings. Even small adjustments, like limiting dining out or cancelling unused subscriptions, can accumulate significant savings over time.

Another practical approach is to establish an emergency savings plan. Families should aim to set aside a specific amount each month, no matter how small, to build a safety net for unexpected expenses. Automating these savings can make the process easier, as funds are transferred directly to a savings account without the temptation to spend. Over time, this fund can provide peace of mind and financial security, helping families navigate unforeseen challenges.

Family Finance Fix: Simple Strategies for Tight Budgets

Meal planning is also a powerful tool for saving money. By planning meals for the week, families can avoid impulse purchases and reduce food waste. Shopping with a list based on planned meals can help stick to a budget, and incorporating more home-cooked meals can significantly lower food costs. Additionally, exploring bulk purchasing and seasonal produce can further enhance savings, making it easier for families to manage their grocery expenses.

Families can also consider generating income from home to bolster their financial situation. This could involve taking on freelance work, selling handmade goods, or even renting out a room. By leveraging skills or resources available at home, families can create additional income streams that contribute to their savings goals. This not only helps alleviate financial stress but also encourages resourcefulness and creativity in tough times.

Lastly, adopting sustainable living practices can lead to long-term savings. Simple changes, such as reducing energy consumption, using public transport, or growing a garden, can significantly cut household costs. By prioritizing sustainability, families not only save money but also contribute positively to their environment. These strategies, when combined, can empower families to build their savings quickly and effectively, fostering a sense of financial stability in challenging times.

"We started growing some of our fruit, vegetables and herbs to which was healthier and cost effective." MJ of FHWM

https://amzn.to/47wd0VS **Weekly Gardening Log**

04

Chapter 4: Strategies for Reducing Household Debt

Understanding Different Types of Debt

Debt can take many forms, and understanding the different types is crucial for anyone facing financial hardship. The most common categories include secured debt, unsecured debt, and revolving debt. Secured debt is backed by collateral, such as a house or car, meaning that failure to repay can result in losing the asset. Unsecured debt, on the other hand, is not tied to any specific asset and includes credit cards and personal loans. This type of debt often comes with higher interest rates and can escalate quickly if not managed properly.

Revolving debt is a subset of unsecured debt, primarily associated with credit cards. It allows borrowers to spend up to a certain limit and pay off the balance over time. However, the flexibility of revolving debt can lead to overspending, making it vital for families to keep track of their limits and ensure they do not accumulate more debt than they can handle. Understanding these categories is essential for developing effective budgeting strategies and emergency savings plans.

Another important type of debt that families often encounter is student loans. With rising education costs, many young adults find themselves burdened with significant debt after graduation. These loans can have various repayment plans, and understanding the terms is essential for managing payments effectively. Families can explore options like income-driven repayment plans or loan forgiveness programs, which can ease the financial strain and help them stay afloat during difficult times.

Medical debt is another significant concern, particularly for those without adequate health insurance. Unexpected medical bills can quickly accumulate, leading to financial distress for families. It's crucial to communicate with healthcare providers about payment plans or financial assistance options available. Families should also consider setting aside emergency savings specifically for medical expenses to prevent these debts from becoming overwhelming. Families can also invest in Health savings accounts when available through employers who will also add money to this account to be used for health-related expenses.

Lastly, it's important to recognize the psychological impact of debt on families. The stress associated with financial hardship can affect mental health and family dynamics. By understanding the types of debt and implementing strategies for reduction, such as meal planning for cost-effective family meals and exploring home-based income generation ideas, families can work towards a more sustainable financial future.

Building a supportive environment where conversations about money are open and constructive can also play a vital role in overcoming debt challenges.

Developing a Debt Repayment Plan

Creating a debt repayment plan is an essential step toward regaining financial stability, especially for families facing economic hardship. The first step is to assess your current financial situation. Gather all your financial documents, including bills, loan statements, and any other debts. This comprehensive overview will help you understand your total debt and identify which debts are the most urgent based on interest rates and payment deadlines.

Once you have a clear picture of your debts, prioritizing them is crucial. Focus on high-interest debts first, such as credit cards, while maintaining minimum payments on others. This strategy not only reduces the total interest paid over time but also helps in creating a structured approach to repayments. Consider using the debt avalanche method, where you pay off debts from highest to lowest interest rates, or the snowball method, which focuses on paying off the smallest debts first to build momentum.

Next, it's vital to develop a budget that accommodates your debt repayment goals. Allocate a specific portion of your monthly income towards debt repayment after covering essential expenses such as housing, food, and utilities. This might require making difficult choices, such as cutting back on discretionary spending or finding ways to increase household income through side jobs or home-based work.

In addition to budgeting, establishing an emergency savings plan can prevent further debt accumulation. Aim to set aside a small amount each month to create a financial cushion for unexpected expenses. This can alleviate the pressure on your budget and allow you to focus on your debt repayment plan without the fear of falling back into debt due to unforeseen circumstances.

Lastly, consider reaching out for support if needed. There are many resources available for families in distress, including financial counselling services and community support groups. These resources can provide valuable advice and help you stay motivated as you work towards becoming debt-free. Remember, developing a debt repayment plan is a journey, and each step taken brings you closer to financial freedom.

Negotiating with Creditors

Negotiating with creditors is an essential skill for anyone facing financial hardship. It is crucial to approach this process with a clear understanding of your financial situation and an honest assessment of what you can afford. Start by gathering all relevant information about your debts, including amounts owed, interest rates, and payment terms. This knowledge will empower you to communicate effectively with your creditors and set realistic goals for negotiation.

When you reach out to creditors, be polite and professional. A positive attitude can go a long way in fostering cooperation. Explain your circumstances and express your willingness to meet your obligations, but also be clear about your limitations. Many creditors are open to negotiation, especially if they see that you are proactive in addressing your debts. It is not uncommon for them to offer reduced rates, extended payment terms, or even debt forgiveness in certain situations.

Consider proposing a repayment plan that aligns with your current financial capabilities. This could involve smaller monthly payments or temporarily pausing payments altogether. To strengthen your case, be prepared to provide documentation of your income and expenses. This transparency can help build trust with your creditors and may lead to more favorable terms. Remember, the goal is to reach a mutually beneficial agreement that allows you to manage your debts without overwhelming financial strain.

It is also wise to be aware of your rights when negotiating with creditors. Familiarize yourself with the Fair Debt Collection Practices Act, which protects consumers from abusive practices. Knowing your rights can help you stand firm during negotiations and ensure that you are treated fairly. If you feel overwhelmed, consider seeking help from a credit counselling service that can guide you through the negotiation process and offer additional strategies for managing your debts.

Finally, keep a record of all communications and agreements made during the negotiation process. This documentation will be invaluable if any disputes arise in the future. By taking proactive steps to negotiate with creditors, you can alleviate some of the financial pressure you are experiencing. With determination and a strategic approach, it is possible to find a path towards financial stability and peace of mind. There are also companies who charge a fee to consolidate and negotiate reduction of multiple debts into one payment on your behalf. This is an option if the number of debtors and amount of debt is overwhelming.

CONTRACT

05

Chapter 5: Meal Planning for Cost-Effective Family Meals

The Benefits of Meal Planning

Meal planning is a powerful strategy that can help families manage their finances more effectively, especially for those facing economic hardship. By taking the time to plan meals, families can avoid impulse purchases and reduce food waste, leading to significant savings over time. This approach not only helps in budgeting but also ensures that families are consuming nutritious meals without overspending. With a little organisation, meal planning can transform how families approach their grocery shopping and cooking routines.

One of the primary benefits of meal planning is the ability to create a shopping list based on planned meals. This targeted approach means families can purchase only what they need, reducing the likelihood of buying unnecessary items that can strain a tight budget. Furthermore, having a list helps in resisting the temptation of purchasing convenience foods, which are often more expensive. By sticking to a plan, families can keep their spending in check and make the most of their limited resources.

Meal planning also allows families to take advantage of sales and seasonal produce. By planning meals around items that are on sale or in season, families can significantly cut down their grocery bills. Bulk buying staples that can be used in multiple meals is another excellent way to save money. This strategy not only aids in budgeting but also promotes a healthier diet by encouraging families to incorporate a variety of foods into their meals, thereby improving nutrition.

Moreover, meal planning fosters creativity in the kitchen and can become a fun family activity. Involving children or other family members in the planning and cooking process can help them learn valuable skills and appreciate the effort that goes into preparing meals. This collaborative approach not only strengthens family bonds but also instils a sense of responsibility regarding food and finances, which is essential for building a sustainable household.

Ultimately, the practice of meal planning is a vital component of financial survival for families in distress. By adopting this strategy, families can not only reduce their food expenses but also cultivate healthier eating habits and strengthen family ties. In today's economic climate, where every penny counts, meal planning stands out as a practical solution for those looking to navigate their financial challenges more effectively.

Creating a Weekly Meal Plan

Creating a weekly meal plan can be a game-changer for families striving to manage their finances effectively. It allows for better budgeting, reducing food waste, and ensuring that meals are nutritious and cost-effective. By dedicating a little time each week to plan, families can save money and improve their overall eating habits. This strategy is particularly beneficial for those facing economic hardship, as it enables them to stretch their food budget further while still enjoying a variety of meals.

Begin by assessing your family's dietary needs and preferences. This understanding will guide you in selecting meals that everyone will enjoy, reducing the chances of food going uneaten. Once you have a grasp of what your family likes, take stock of what you already have in your pantry and refrigerator. This step not only helps in minimizing waste but also allows you to incorporate existing ingredients into your meal plans, making it a more economical approach.

Next, create a balanced meal plan that incorporates a variety of food groups. Aim for a mix of proteins, vegetables, grains, and healthy fats. This variety ensures that your family receives essential nutrients while keeping meals interesting. Consider using bulk ingredients and seasonal produce, which are often cheaper and can be used in multiple recipes throughout the week.

Once the meal plan is established, prepare a shopping list to ensure you only purchase what is necessary. Sticking to this list can significantly cut down on impulse buys and help you stay within your budget. Additionally, try to shop at local markets or discount stores where fresh produce and staples might be available at lower prices. This approach not only supports your budget but also promotes community-based shopping, which can be more sustainable.

Finally, involve your family in the meal preparation process. Engaging everyone in cooking can be both fun and educational, teaching children valuable skills while fostering teamwork. Meal prepping on weekends can also save time during busy weekdays, allowing for quick, healthy meals. By incorporating these strategies, families can create a weekly meal plan that is not only cost-effective but also promotes better nutrition and family bonding, essential components for those in financial distress.

Shopping Smart: Tips for Saving on Groceries

Shopping for groceries can often feel overwhelming, especially for families facing economic hardships. However, with a few smart strategies, it is possible to make your grocery budget stretch further. Start by creating a detailed shopping list based on meal planning for the week. This not only helps in avoiding impulse purchases but also ensures you have all the ingredients needed for cost-effective family meals, reducing the likelihood of food waste.

Another effective way to save on groceries is by taking advantage of sales and discounts. Keep an eye on local supermarket flyers and apps that offer coupons. Many stores have loyalty programs that provide discounts on frequently purchased items. By combining these offers with your shopping list, you can significantly reduce your overall spending. Additionally, consider shopping at discount stores or local farmers' markets, where prices may be lower than big chain supermarkets.

Buying in bulk can also lead to substantial savings over time. Non-perishable items like rice, pasta, and canned goods can often be bought at a lower price per unit when purchased in larger quantities. Just ensure that the items you choose are ones your family will consume before they expire. This strategy not only reduces the cost per item but also helps in stocking up for emergencies, contributing to a family's emergency savings plan.

Moreover, cooking at home rather than eating out is a vital strategy in managing household finances. Preparing meals from scratch can be more economical and healthier. Try to involve the entire family in meal preparation, which can also be a fun way to bond. Look for simple recipes that use affordable ingredients, and consider batch cooking to save time and energy during the week.

Finally, consider exploring home-based income generation ideas to supplement your grocery budget. This could include selling homemade goods or offering services such as babysitting or tutoring. Finding ways to earn extra income can provide more financial breathing room and help alleviate some of the stress associated with tight budgets. With these strategies, families can not only survive but thrive, even in challenging economic times.

06

Chapter 6: Home-Based Income Generation Ideas

Identifying Skills and Talents

Identifying skills and talents is a crucial step for families facing economic hardship, as these assets can open doors to new opportunities. Many individuals possess untapped skills, whether they be cooking, crafting, or technical abilities. Recognizing these talents allows families to navigate financial challenges more effectively and can lead to potential income sources. By assessing what each family member excels at, households can create a plan that leverages these strengths for financial improvement.

The first step in identifying skills is to conduct a family skills inventory. This process involves sitting down together and discussing what each person feels they are good at or enjoys doing. It's important to create an open environment where everyone feels comfortable sharing their thoughts. This inventory can reveal surprising talents that may not have been previously considered, such as gardening skills that could lead to a small produce business or crafting abilities that can be turned into saleable products.

Once the family has compiled a list of skills, the next phase is to explore how these talents can translate into financial opportunities. For instance, if someone has a knack for cooking, they might consider starting a meal prep service for busy families. Alternatively, if there are strong organizational skills within the family, they could offer to help others with budgeting or household management. By creatively thinking about how these skills can serve others, families can tap into new income streams.

In addition to income generation, identifying skills can significantly enhance a family's budgeting strategies. Understanding what talents can be used to save money is just as important as recognizing those that can earn it. For example, if a family member can sew, they can repair clothing instead of purchasing new items. This not only cuts costs but also encourages sustainable living by reducing waste. Integrating skills into daily life can lead to a more frugal lifestyle that alleviates financial stress.

Lastly, it's essential to regularly revisit and update the skills inventory as family members grow and develop new talents. This ongoing process allows families to adapt to changing circumstances and continue to find innovative ways to manage their finances. By embracing the skills and talents within the household, families can create a resilient and resourceful approach to overcoming financial difficulties, ultimately paving the way for a more secure future.

In today's rapidly changing economic landscape, remote work opportunities have emerged as a viable solution for families facing financial challenges. This shift in the workplace allows individuals to explore job options that were previously inaccessible due to geographical constraints. By tapping into the remote job market, families can find flexible employment that accommodates their existing responsibilities, making it easier to balance work and home life, especially for those with children or elderly family members to care for.

Remote work not only provides a source of income but also offers the potential for significant savings on commuting and related expenses. Families can cut down on costs associated with travelling to and from work, such as fuel, public transport fares, and even work attire. This can be particularly beneficial for families in financial distress, as every penny saved contributes to a more sustainable budget, allowing them to allocate funds towards essential needs or emergency savings.

Exploring Remote Work Opportunities

Moreover, the variety of remote work available caters to diverse skill sets and interests. Whether it's freelance writing, virtual assistance, or customer service roles, there are countless opportunities that can be tailored to fit individual strengths. Families can leverage existing skills or even pursue new ones through online courses, making them more attractive candidates in the competitive remote job market. This adaptability is crucial in today's economy, where job security may be uncertain.

In addition to traditional remote jobs, families might consider home-based income generation ideas such as starting a small business or engaging in gig economy tasks. These options not only provide financial relief but also allow families to work together, strengthening bonds while contributing to the household income. Activities such as crafting, baking, or offering services like tutoring can turn hobbies into profitable ventures, making the most of available resources.

Lastly, embracing a mindset of sustainable living can further enhance the benefits of remote work. By reducing household costs through mindful spending and efficient budgeting strategies, families can create a more resilient financial future. Remote work, combined with a commitment to sustainability and cost-effective practices, empowers families to navigate economic hardships with greater confidence and stability. This holistic approach can lead to improved financial health and a more harmonious family life in challenging times.

Starting a Home-Based Business

Starting a home-based business can be a viable solution for families facing economic hardship. It allows you to generate income while managing your household responsibilities. The flexibility of working from home means you can tailor your hours to fit around family commitments, making it an excellent option for young adults and elderly individuals alike. By leveraging your skills and interests, you can turn a passion into a profitable venture, providing both financial relief and personal satisfaction.

To begin, assess your skills and interests to identify potential business ideas. Consider what services or products you can offer that align with your expertise and the needs of your community. This could range from freelance writing, graphic design, or tutoring to crafting handmade goods. Researching market demands can help you refine your business concept, ensuring that it is both relevant and profitable. A solid plan will guide your efforts and increase your chances of success.

Budgeting is crucial when starting a home-based business. You should outline your initial costs, including materials, marketing, and any necessary equipment. This will help you understand the financial commitment involved and allow you to allocate resources effectively. Additionally, setting realistic income goals will keep you motivated while ensuring your business remains sustainable. Remember, it may take time to see significant profits, so patience and persistence are key.

Creating a dedicated workspace within your home can enhance productivity and professionalism. A specific area for work helps eliminate distractions and signals to family members that you are in 'work mode'. This can be a simple desk or a more elaborate setup, depending on your space and budget. Moreover, establishing a routine can help you balance work and family life effectively, ensuring that neither is neglected.

Finally, consider utilizing online platforms for marketing your business. Social media, websites, and local community boards can be excellent tools for reaching potential customers. Engage with your audience, share your story, and showcase your products or services. Building a network of support among fellow home-based business owners can also provide valuable insights and encouragement. With determination and strategic planning, starting a home-based business can significantly alleviate financial pressures for families in distress.

Set up your home office to start your home-based business.

AUDIENCE

07

Some of the Fun Home-Based Businesses started by MJ of FHWM:

FHWM-retail.myshopify.com
has frequent pop-up shops
during health conferences,
social events, seasonal markets & more
Email us for questions and
requests at fhwmretail@gmail.com

Blog-style Website by MJ of FHWM
for affiliate marketing and
FHWM Brand products and resources

betterbuyinsider.com

https://fhwmretail.org

on-line faith-based merch store

some faith-based merch

available during pop-up events

Season&Grace Co
FAITH ART & STYLE IN EVERY SEASON

I design and
develop
experiences
that make
people's lives
simple.

08

Chapter 7: Sustainable Living to Cut Household Costs

Embracing Minimalism

Embracing minimalism is not just a lifestyle choice; it is a powerful approach to managing household finances, especially for families facing economic hardship. By focusing on the essentials and reducing unnecessary expenditures, families can alleviate financial stress and create a more sustainable living environment. This shift in mindset encourages individuals to evaluate their needs versus wants, paving the way for smarter budgeting strategies that prioritize financial security over material possessions.

One of the key benefits of adopting a minimalist approach is the ability to streamline household expenses. Families can begin by decluttering their living spaces, which often leads to the discovery of items that are no longer needed or used. Selling or donating these items not only provides extra cash but also fosters a sense of accomplishment and clarity. This process helps families focus on what truly matters, allowing them to allocate funds towards emergency savings plans and debt reduction strategies.

Meal planning is another practical aspect of minimalism that can significantly impact a family's budget. By preparing a weekly menu and shopping list based on essential ingredients, families can avoid impulse purchases and reduce food waste. This approach not only saves money but also encourages healthier eating habits. Cooking at home using simple, cost-effective recipes can create a sense of togetherness and strengthen family bonds while promoting financial discipline.

In addition to managing expenses, minimalism also opens the door to home-based income generation ideas for families. By utilizing skills and resources already available, families can explore side hustles such as selling handmade crafts, providing tutoring services, or offering online freelance work. These ventures not only contribute to household income but also encourage creativity and resourcefulness, helping families to thrive amidst financial challenges.

Ultimately, embracing minimalism is about adopting a sustainable lifestyle that prioritizes financial well-being and emotional resilience. By reducing clutter, simplifying meal planning, and exploring new income opportunities, families can cultivate a sense of control over their finances. This holistic approach not only aids in surviving economic distress but also fosters a deeper appreciation for the simple joys of life, leading to a more fulfilling and balanced existence.

Energy and Water Conservation Techniques

In today's economic climate, conserving energy and water is not just an environmentally responsible choice; it's a crucial strategy for families facing financial hardship. By implementing simple energy-saving techniques, households can significantly reduce their monthly utility bills. Simple actions such as switching to energy-efficient bulbs, unplugging devices when not in use, and optimizing heating and cooling systems can collectively lead to substantial savings. Moreover, using programmable thermostats can help ensure that energy is not wasted when the home is unoccupied or during the night.

Water conservation is equally important and can lead to significant reductions in costs for families. Simple adjustments like fixing leaks, installing low-flow showerheads, and being mindful of water usage during daily activities can lead to lower water bills. Additionally, families can consider rainwater harvesting systems for gardening and other non-potable uses, which not only saves money but also promotes sustainable living practices. Every drop saved contributes directly to financial relief and resource conservation.

Meal planning can also intertwine with energy and water conservation techniques. Preparing meals in bulk can save energy by reducing the number of times the stove or oven is used, and it can also help minimize food waste. Families can plan meals around seasonal produce, which is often fresher, more affordable, and requires less energy for transportation. By combining efficient meal preparation with energy conservation, households can stretch their budgets further while enjoying healthier meals.

Another effective strategy for families in financial distress is to engage in community efforts focused on conservation. Local workshops on sustainable practices often provide families with valuable information and resources on how to save both energy and money. Participating in community exchanges or co-ops can also lead to shared resources, enabling families to acquire necessary items without incurring significant expenses. Such community engagement fosters not only practical skills but also a support network during tough economic times.

Ultimately, the combined approach of energy and water conservation techniques can lead to a more sustainable and financially stable household. Families that actively implement these practices will not only see immediate financial benefits but also contribute to a healthier environment. Embracing these strategies fosters a sense of responsibility and empowerment, allowing families to navigate economic hardships with resilience and creativity.

Growing Your Own Food

Growing your own food can significantly alleviate financial strain, especially for families in economic hardship. By cultivating a garden, whether it's in a backyard, on a balcony, or even in pots, you can provide fresh produce for your household, reducing grocery bills. This practice not only helps in saving money but also promotes healthier eating habits, as homegrown vegetables and fruits are often more nutritious than store-bought alternatives.

In addition to the direct financial benefits, growing your own food can be a rewarding and educational experience for the entire family. It offers a wonderful opportunity for children to learn about nature, responsibility, and the importance of sustainability. Involving the entire family in gardening activities can strengthen bonds, enhance teamwork, and instill a sense of accomplishment as you watch your plants flourish.

For those who may feel daunted by the idea of gardening, starting small is key. Begin with easy-to-grow vegetables such as tomatoes, lettuce, or herbs, which require minimal space and effort. Container gardening is also a viable option for those with limited outdoor space. With some basic supplies, such as soil, pots, and seeds, you can create a thriving garden that will yield produce throughout the growing season.

Moreover, growing your own food can lead to greater financial independence in the long run. By becoming more self-sufficient, families can reduce their reliance on expensive grocery stores and the volatile market prices of food. This not only helps in managing household budgets but also opens up new opportunities for home-based income generation. Surplus produce can be sold or traded, providing a small income while fostering community relationships.

Finally, integrating sustainable living practices into your gardening efforts can further enhance your financial strategy. Composting kitchen scraps, using rainwater for irrigation, and employing organic pest control methods can all contribute to reducing household costs. By embracing the principles of sustainability, families can create a more resilient and financially stable future, all while enjoying the benefits of fresh, homegrown food.

"We use all vegetable and fruit scraps in our compost bin to enrich our garden soil." MJ of FHWM

09

Chapter 8: Resources and Tools for Financial Management

Budgeting Apps and Tools

In today's challenging economic climate, budgeting apps and tools have become essential for families striving to manage their finances effectively. These digital resources simplify tracking income and expenses, allowing users to gain a clear picture of their financial situation. For families facing economic hardship, having a structured budget can make a significant difference in their ability to survive and thrive, providing peace of mind and direction amidst financial uncertainty.

One of the most popular budgeting tools is the mobile app, designed to cater to various needs and preferences. Many of these apps offer features that allow users to set spending limits, monitor transactions, and even create savings goals. For the elderly or those unfamiliar with technology, user-friendly interfaces and customer support can help make the transition to digital budgeting smoother, ensuring that everyone can take advantage of these helpful tools.

Additionally, budgeting apps often come with educational resources that empower families to make informed financial decisions. These resources may include articles, videos, or interactive tutorials that explain budgeting strategies, emergency savings plans, and methods for reducing household debt. By understanding these concepts, families can build a stronger financial foundation and develop sustainable living practices that cut costs while improving their quality of life.

Meal planning is another area where budgeting tools can shine. Many apps allow users to create shopping lists based on planned meals, helping families to avoid overspending at the grocery store. By focusing on cost-effective family meals and maximizing the use of pantry staples, families can stretch their food budgets further and minimize waste, which is especially vital during times of financial distress.

Finally, some budgeting apps offer features that assist in identifying potential home-based income generation ideas. By analyzing spending habits and suggesting areas for potential savings, these tools can also highlight opportunities for families to earn extra income from home. As families embrace these budgeting strategies, they not only work towards financial stability but also foster a sense of community and support among those experiencing similar hardships, creating a network of resilience in challenging times.

Community Resources and Support

In times of economic hardship, community resources and support systems play a vital role in helping families navigate through financial difficulties. Local organizations, non-profits, and government agencies often provide essential services such as food banks, financial counselling, and educational workshops. Families facing financial distress can significantly benefit from these resources, as they not only address immediate needs but also offer guidance on long-term financial management and survival strategies.

Budgeting strategies are crucial for families looking to regain control over their finances. Community workshops often teach practical skills, such as how to create a household budget, track expenses, and priorities spending. By participating in these sessions, families can learn to identify areas where they can cut costs and make informed decisions about their financial future. Furthermore, sharing experiences with others in similar situations can provide emotional support and motivation.

Emergency savings plans are another essential aspect of financial stability. Many community organizations encourage families to set up emergency funds to cover unexpected expenses. Financial advisors often recommend saving at least three to six months' worth of living expenses. Local communities can assist by providing resources that facilitate savings, such as matched savings programs, and offering workshops that focus on the importance of financial preparedness.

Reducing household debt is a common challenge for families in economic hardship. Community resources often include debt management programs that offer free or low-cost services to help families negotiate with creditors and develop structured repayment plans. Access to these services can alleviate the stress of overwhelming debt and provide a clear path towards financial recovery. Additionally, support groups can help families stay accountable and motivated throughout their journey to becoming debt-free.

Meal planning is another practical strategy that families can utilize to cut costs. Many community centers host cooking classes and nutrition workshops that teach families how to prepare healthy, cost-effective meals. By learning to meal plan effectively, families can reduce food waste, save money, and ensure they are providing nutritious options for their loved ones. Home-based income generation ideas, such as starting a small business or engaging in freelance work, can further bolster a family's financial situation, providing them with additional resources to navigate through tough times.

Educational Resources for Ongoing Learning

In the current economic climate, ongoing learning is essential for individuals and families facing financial hardships. Accessing educational resources can empower you with the knowledge necessary to manage household finances more effectively. Various online platforms offer free or low-cost courses on budgeting strategies, helping families understand how to allocate their resources wisely and reduce unnecessary expenses. Additionally, local community centers often host workshops focused on financial literacy, providing invaluable insights into managing money and planning for emergencies.

Meal planning is another area where education can significantly impact financial stability. Families can benefit from learning how to prepare cost-effective meals that not only save money but also promote healthier eating habits. Resources such as cookbooks, blogs, and online videos can guide families through creating budget-friendly meal plans that reduce food waste and ensure nutritious food is available for all family members. Understanding how to shop smartly and utilize seasonal produce can further enhance these efforts.

For those looking to generate additional income, various online courses and webinars are available that focus on home-based income generation ideas. These resources can introduce families to side hustles, freelancing opportunities, and entrepreneurship. By exploring these avenues, families can supplement their income, thereby alleviating some of the financial pressures they may face. Learning how to market skills or crafts online can open new doors for economic opportunities.

Another crucial aspect of ongoing learning is understanding the principles of sustainable living. There is a wealth of information available on how to cut household costs through eco-friendly practices. Families can learn about energy conservation, water-saving techniques, and DIY projects that enhance home efficiency while saving money. Educational resources in this area not only provide financial benefits but also contribute to a healthier planet, making sustainability a worthwhile investment for the future.

Lastly, many libraries offer free access to financial advisory services and workshops designed to assist families in developing emergency savings plans and strategies for reducing household debt. These resources can help families navigate their financial challenges more effectively, providing tailored advice and support. Engaging with these educational opportunities can foster a proactive approach to financial management, equipping families with the tools they need to thrive even in tough economic times.

Chapter 9: Maintaining Financial Health Long-Term

Reviewing and Adjusting Your Budget

Reviewing and adjusting your budget is a vital step for families facing economic hardship. It allows you to take a closer look at your spending habits and identify areas where you can make necessary changes. Regularly reviewing your budget not only helps in tracking your financial progress but also ensures that you remain aligned with your financial goals. In times of financial distress, being proactive about your budget can be the difference between sinking and staying afloat.

Start by evaluating your current expenses. Categorize them into essential and non-essential spending. Essential expenses include rent, utilities, groceries, and healthcare, while non-essential expenses might encompass dining out, subscriptions, and entertainment. By distinguishing between these categories, you can pinpoint where cuts can be made without significantly impacting your quality of life. This assessment is crucial for families, particularly those with children, as it helps prioritize spending on necessities while identifying areas to economize.

Once you have a clear view of your expenditures, it's time to set new, realistic financial goals. These goals should be specific, measurable, achievable, relevant, and time-bound (SMART). For instance, aim to reduce your grocery budget by 20% over the next three months or set aside a specific amount for emergency savings each month. By establishing clear goals, you can create a focused plan that encourages family participation in budgeting efforts, making it a team endeavor.

Incorporate strategies for reducing household debt into your budget review. This may involve consolidating loans, negotiating lower interest rates, or prioritizing high-interest debts. Families can also benefit from exploring home-based income generation ideas, such as starting a small side business or offering services within the community. This not only provides additional income but can also foster a sense of unity and purpose as family members work towards common financial goals.

Lastly, consider meal planning as an effective tool for cost-effective family meals. By planning your meals in advance, you can utilize ingredients efficiently and minimize waste. This not only saves money but also promotes healthier eating habits. Sustainable living practices, such as growing your own vegetables or reducing energy consumption, can further cut household costs. Reviewing and adjusting your budget regularly ensures that you adapt to changing circumstances, maintain financial stability, and foster a resilient household.

Setting New Financial Goals

Setting new financial goals is essential for families facing economic hardship. By reassessing your current financial situation, you can identify areas that need improvement and set realistic targets that can lead to financial stability. It is important to involve all family members in this process, as shared goals foster a sense of teamwork and accountability. Begin by discussing your family's values and priorities to ensure that everyone is on the same page and motivated to achieve these goals together.

Once you have established your family's financial values, it is time to set specific, measurable, achievable, relevant, and time-bound (SMART) goals. For instance, instead of stating that you want to save money, specify the amount you aim to save within a certain timeframe. This could be saving $500 for an emergency fund within six months. Setting such clear objectives allows you to track your progress and adjust your strategies as needed, ensuring you stay committed to your financial journey.

To support your financial goals, create a detailed budget that outlines your income, expenses, and savings targets. A well-structured budget will help you identify unnecessary expenditures and areas where you can cut costs. For families in financial distress, prioritizing essential spending while adopting frugal habits, such as meal planning and reducing entertainment costs, can significantly contribute to meeting your goals. Regularly reviewing and adjusting your budget will also keep your financial plan aligned with changing circumstances.

In addition to budgeting, building an emergency savings plan is crucial for managing unexpected expenses. Aim to set aside a small portion of your income each month to create a safety net for your family. This can prevent further financial strain when emergencies arise, such as medical bills or car repairs. Even a modest emergency fund can provide peace of mind and stability during challenging times, allowing your family to focus on achieving broader financial objectives.

Finally, consider exploring home-based income generation ideas that can supplement your family's earnings. This could involve turning hobbies into side businesses or finding flexible work-from-home opportunities. By diversifying your income sources and being proactive about financial challenges, you can empower your family to take control of your financial future, ultimately leading to a more secure and sustainable household. Embracing these strategies will help you set and achieve new financial goals, paving the way toward a brighter economic outlook for your family.

Building Wealth for the Future

Building wealth for the future is an essential goal for families facing economic hardships. It is crucial to establish a financial foundation that not only addresses immediate needs but also prepares for long-term stability. This involves creating a realistic budget that accounts for all household income and expenses, ensuring that every dollar is allocated wisely. By prioritizing essential costs and identifying areas where cuts can be made, families can redirect funds towards savings and debt reduction, paving the way for a more secure financial future.

One of the key strategies for families is developing an emergency savings plan. Setting aside even a small amount each month can lead to a significant safety net over time. This fund can help cover unexpected expenses without resorting to credit cards or loans, which often lead to further financial strain. Families should aim for at least three to six months' worth of living expenses in their emergency fund, which provides peace of mind and a cushion during tough times.

Reducing household debt is another critical aspect of building wealth. Families should assess their current debts and prioritize paying off high-interest loans first. This can be achieved through various methods, such as the snowball method, where smaller debts are paid off first to create momentum, or the avalanche method, which focuses on debts with the highest interest rates. Additionally, families can seek professional advice on debt management plans that may offer relief without further financial burden.

Meal planning is a practical strategy that can significantly reduce household costs. By planning meals for the week and shopping with a list, families can avoid impulse buys and minimize food waste. This not only saves money but also encourages healthier eating habits. Incorporating bulk purchases and seasonal produce can further enhance savings, allowing families to enjoy nutritious meals without overspending.

Finally, exploring home-based income generation ideas can provide a much-needed boost to a family's finances. From freelance work to starting a small home business, there are numerous opportunities to supplement income. Families can leverage skills they already possess or explore new avenues that fit their lifestyle. Embracing sustainable living practices, such as gardening or DIY projects, can also cut costs and promote self-sufficiency, ultimately contributing to a brighter financial future.

💛 Building Hope, One Family at a Time

In times like these, when every dollar feels stretched and uncertainty seems to shadow every plan, I want you to remember this: you are not alone, and your situation is not hopeless. Every small, faithful step you take toward financial health — whether that's cooking at home, planting a small garden, or starting a side business from your kitchen table — is an act of courage and stewardship. When I first began exploring home-based businesses, I didn't have all the answers. I simply started where I was — creating, learning, and praying over every idea. From my FHWM Retail Store on Shopify to Season & Grace Co. on Etsy, creating on FHWM with Marcy on YouTube and even the affiliate website BetterBuyInsider.com

platform, each venture began as a way to serve others while supporting my family.

These aren't just stores; they're reminders that we can turn faith and creativity into opportunity. You, too, can do the same. Maybe it's selling handmade items, repurposing what you already own, or using the simple budgeting tools and worksheets found in my Amazon books and FHWM resources. Perhaps it's growing vegetables to save on groceries, or joining a local community group to share and trade what you each have. Each of these steps matters — not only for your finances, but for your faith, your health, and your family's future. My heart behind Family Finance Fix and all of FHWM Retail is to help families thrive again — to replace fear with faith, and lack with lasting wisdom.

Whether you're tightening your budget, exploring new income ideas, or simply trying to breathe easier about tomorrow, know that you have a sister in this journey who believes in your ability to rebuild. Together, through faith, health, wellness, and meaningful motivation, we can strengthen not just our budgets — but our entire community.

🌿 *With Faith and Hope,*

Marcy "MJ" Anderson Founder, FHWM Retail & BetterBuyInsider.com

Encouraging families to live well, grow your faith in God, give grace, and thrive in every season.

Resources & Tools by Marcy "MJ" Anderson of FHV

Faith • Health • Wellness • Motivation

Below are trusted tools and resources created to he strengthen your faith, health, finances and overall w Each one is designed to help you live well, spend w grounded in faith through every season.

🛍️ Visit: https://fhwm-retail.myshopify.com

💼 FHWM Retail — Home of Faith-Based Health & Wellness Shop nurse-approved products that promote healthy, active living for the whole family.

🕊️ **Season & Grace Co on Etsy**

Faith-inspired decor, candles, wall art, and apparel designed to bring peace and purpose into your home — beautifully and uniquely. ✨ Visit: https://www.etsy.com/shop/SeasonandGraceCo

BetterBuyInsider.com. Discover smart deals, family-friendly finds, and affordable lifestyle products-all curated with real wellness and real cost-effectiveness in mind.

🌿 Explore: https://betterbuyinsider.com

📚 Books by Marcy Anderson Faith-forward guides and practical planners to help you manage your home, health, and finances with grace and confidence. ■ Find on Amazon: Search "Marcy Anderson Journals FHWM Retail"

🎥 FHWM with Marcy YouTube Channel
Join our growing community for weekly encouragement, wellness trends, and motivational messages that blend faith, health, and real-life inspiration. ▶️ Watch: FHWM with Marcy on YouTube

🌸**Community & Coaching Interested in community events, wellness workshops, or speaking engagements? Reach out to collaborate or learn more about upcoming initiatives that support families in faith, health, and financial resilience. 📩 Email: fhwmretail@gmail.com**

✨ *"Every home can become a place of faith, strength, and restoration. Start where you are, use what you have, and trust that God's grace will do the rest."* — Marcy "MJ" Anderson

This book addressed the easy steps that can be immediately implemented to make a difference in a family's financial health and survival during these challenging times. There are many other steps that families can explore after the basics have been completed and maintained. Individuals can find financial/business mentors, learn the stock market, learn tax saving strategies, take free workshops at community colleges, churches, libraries, Home Depot, etc. when available for learning a new skill and more. All of the suggestions provided in this book are to be repeated, re-evaluated, adjusted as your situation, economy and family needs.

Family Finance...

Discover practical strategies to navigate tight budgets with "Family Finance Fix." This essential guide empowers families to make informed financial decisions, from meal planning and generating home-based income to establishing emergency savings and managing debt. With actionable insights and a focus on sustainability, it transforms financial distress into a path toward stability and prosperity.

Some Helpful Tools

To do list

Start to plan your goals based on the tips you learned

In 6 months from now I want to achieve...

What do I want to accomplish?

What is important to me?

Insights

Feel free to write down any after-reading insights and thoughts

In 6 months from now I want to achieve...

- ________________________________
- ________________________________
- ________________________________
- ________________________________
- ________________________________

Table

Fill your data

Title	Title	Title	Title	Title	Title
1					
2					
3					
4					
5					
6					

- Tax Deduction -

- [ ]
- [ ]
- [ ]
- [ ]
- [ ]
- [ ]
- [ ]
- [ ]
- [ ]
- [ ]
- [ ]
- [ ]
- [ ]
- [ ]
- [ ]
- [ ]
- [ ]
- [ ]
- [ ]
- [ ]
- [ ]
- [ ]
- [ ]
- [ ]
- [ ]
- [ ]
- [ ]
- [ ]
- [ ]
- [ ]
- [ ]
- [ ]
- [ ]
- [ ]
- [ ]
- [ ]
- [ ]
- [ ]
- [ ]
- [ ]
- [ ]
- [ ]
- [ ]
- [ ]
- [ ]
- [ ]
- [ ]
- [ ]

EXPENSES

DATE	EXPENSE TYPE	CATEGORY	METHOD	AMOUNT
			TOTAL:	

EXPENSES

DATE	EXPENSE TYPE	CATEGORY	METHOD	AMOUNT
			TOTAL:	

EXPENSES

DATE	EXPENSE TYPE	CATEGORY	METHOD	AMOUNT
			TOTAL:	

EXPENSES

DATE	EXPENSE TYPE	CATEGORY	METHOD	AMOUNT
			TOTAL:	

EXPENSES

DATE	EXPENSE TYPE	CATEGORY	METHOD	AMOUNT
			TOTAL:	

SAVING TRACKER

SAVING FOR:

DATE	DEPOSIT	AMOUNT

SAVING FOR:

DATE	DEPOSIT	AMOUNT

SAVING TRACKER

SAVING FOR:

DATE	DEPOSIT	AMOUNT

SAVING FOR:

DATE	DEPOSIT	AMOUNT

SAVING TRACKER

SAVING FOR:

DATE	DEPOSIT	AMOUNT

SAVING FOR:

DATE	DEPOSIT	AMOUNT

SAVING TRACKER

SAVING FOR:

DATE	DEPOSIT	AMOUNT

SAVING FOR:

DATE	DEPOSIT	AMOUNT

SAVING TRACKER

SAVING FOR:

DATE	DEPOSIT	AMOUNT

SAVING FOR:

DATE	DEPOSIT	AMOUNT

DEBT TRACKER

ACCOUNT:

MINIMUM:

DUE DATE:

CREDIT LIMIT:

INTEREST RATE:

ACCOUNT ID:

PASSWORD:

BALANCE	PAYMENT	DATE	NEW BALANCE

DEBT TRACKER

ACCOUNT: ______________________

MINIMUM: ______________________ DUE DATE: ______________________

CREDIT LIMIT: ______________________ INTEREST RATE: ______________________

ACCOUNT ID: ______________________ PASSWORD: ______________________

BALANCE	PAYMENT	DATE	NEW BALANCE

DEBT TRACKER

ACCOUNT:

MINIMUM:

DUE DATE:

CREDIT LIMIT:

INTEREST RATE:

ACCOUNT ID:

PASSWORD:

BALANCE	PAYMENT	DATE	NEW BALANCE

DEBT TRACKER

ACCOUNT:

MINIMUM:

DUE DATE:

CREDIT LIMIT:

INTEREST RATE:

ACCOUNT ID:

PASSWORD:

BALANCE	PAYMENT	DATE	NEW BALANCE

DEBT TRACKER

ACCOUNT:

MINIMUM:

DUE DATE:

CREDIT LIMIT:

INTEREST RATE:

ACCOUNT ID:

PASSWORD:

BALANCE	PAYMENT	DATE	NEW BALANCE

To-Do List

MONTHLY TO-DO LIST

JANUARY

FEBRUARY

MARCH

APRIL

MAY

JUNE

JULY

AUGUST

SEPTEMBER

OCTOBER

NOVEMBER

DECEMBER

To-Do List

MONTHLY TO-DO LIST

JANUARY	FEBRUARY	MARCH
☐	☐	☐
☐	☐	☐
☐	☐	☐
☐	☐	☐
☐	☐	☐

APRIL	MAY	JUNE
☐	☐	☐
☐	☐	☐
☐	☐	☐
☐	☐	☐
☐	☐	☐

JULY	AUGUST	SEPTEMBER
☐	☐	☐
☐	☐	☐
☐	☐	☐
☐	☐	☐
☐	☐	☐

OCTOBER	NOVEMBER	DECEMBER
☐	☐	☐
☐	☐	☐
☐	☐	☐
☐	☐	☐
☐	☐	☐

To-Do List

MONTHLY TO-DO LIST

JANUARY

FEBRUARY

MARCH

APRIL

MAY

JUNE

JULY

AUGUST

SEPTEMBER

OCTOBER

NOVEMBER

DECEMBER

www.ingramcontent.com/pod-product-compliance
Lightning Source LLC
LaVergne TN
LVHW070911210926
848482LV00017B/1045

* 9 7 9 8 3 4 9 6 8 0 7 1 7 *